A LEAF, A FLOWER, A FRUIT, OR EVEN WATER,

OFFERED TO ME IN DEVOTION,

I WILL ACCEPT AS THE LOVING GIFT OF A DEDICATED HEART.

WHATEVER YOU DO, MAKE IT AN OFFERING TO ME;

THE FOOD YOU EAT OR WORSHIP YOU PERFORM,

THE HELP YOU GIVE, EVEN YOUR SUFFERING.

THUS WILL YOU BE FREE FROM KARMA'S BONDAGE,

FROM THE RESULT OF ACTIONS, GOOD AND BAD.

Bhagavad-Gita

છ

HAPPY BELLY HAPPY SOUL
a guide to vedic cooking

by APARNA KHANOLKAR

With loving thanks to:
Sarojini Khanolkar for planting the seed of food and cooking,
Pushpa and **Anand Khanolkar** for nurturing it,
Anjali and **Ben Khanolkar** for patiently witnessing its growth,
Rohit and Anagha and hundreds of clients for
savoring the food and supporting me,

And most of all to Mother Divine for Shakti!

FOREWORD

WHEN DIET IS WRONG, MEDICINE IS OF NO USE.
WHEN DIET IS CORRECT, MEDICINE IS OF NO NEED.

~FROM THE *CHARAKA SAMHITA*, ONE OF THE MOST ANCIENT AND VENERATED AYURVEDIC TEXTBOOKS.

According to Ayurveda, food is more than food. Food is medicine, yet it is more than even medicine; it is life itself. Whatever we eat actually becomes us—in body, mind and spirit. Our food and how we prepare and enjoy it represents the giving and receiving of love; food brings us together in community, it unites families. Food not only represents love, it is love.

Aparna Khanolkar, the Mistress of Spice, understands the essence of this love affair. In the following guide, she says, "Cook with reverence because you are taking care of your health and well-being. It is one of the greatest acts of self-nurturance." These are more than words for Aparna. Whenever she prepares food, shares a recipe or teaches the art of cooking, she does so with a powerful sense of the sacred nature of this ritual.

While the rituals of cooking and preparing food are beautiful and meaningful, in actual practice, these can sometimes be intimidating, even for those who love to eat. They can be more so when considering the art of cooking according to the principles and precepts of Ayurveda. For the uninitiated, the world of Ayurveda can some-times feel like an alchemical mystery, fraught with symbols and esoteric terms, unfamiliar spices and herbal concoctions. Yet, the essence of Ayurveda as a system helps us to cultivate a closer relationship with the cycles of nature that surround us and are found in each and every breath, every bite and every meal.

Aparna knows these secrets well and knows how to demystify them. Her work in person and in these 108 recipes serve up a feast that anyone can prepare as she is a guide who gives instructions anyone can follow—no degree in magic necessary. The beating heart of the science of Ayurveda finds its finest rhythm in the kitchen, and Aparna is a master chef, teacher, recipe creator and guide who knows how to support anyone through the process of creating food that truly embodies love.

~Felicia Marie Tomasko, RN.
EDITOR-IN-CHIEF OF *LA YOGA* AND
AYURVEDA AND HEALTH MAGAZINES. PRESIDENT,
CALIFORNIA ASSOCIATION OF AYURVEDIC MEDICINE,
BOARD OF DIRECTORS, NATIONAL AYURVEDIC
MEDICAL ASSOCIATION

What is vedic cooking?

THE BODY IS THE TEMPLE OF YOUR SOUL. Vedic food is medicinal in nature and is designed to nuture the temple so that your soul may evolve to higher states of consciousness. Vedic cooking is both an art and science. It is an art form because the food is pleasing to all the senses and a science because it does not subscribe to the on-diet-for-all theory, and focuses on healing and balancing the doshas.

Ayurveda states that health is not simply a lack symptoms of disease in the physiology. According to Ayurveda, a healthy person is one whose doshas are balanced, whose channels are open with proper flow of energy, whose wastes are eliminated regularly and one who is radiant and blissful and has an overall sense of health and vitality.

Doshas are principles that govern the body/mind of every individual. These principles are derived from the panchamahabhutas or five elements namely air, space, earth, water and fire. Air and space known as Vata dosha governs the nervous system, and movement including respiration, childbirth and elimination. Pitta dosha is responsible for digestion and metabolism and is governed by fire and water. Kapha dosha is made up of water and earth and is responsible for immunity and mucus production.

When one understands the importance of balancing doshas, it is easy and simple to apply Ayurvedic principles to everyday life. The principle of opposites applies very well in pacifying doshas. Since vata is composed of air and space, which tends to be cold, dry and rough, it is important to pacify it with warm and unctuous foods. Pitta, which is fiery, is pacified with cooling foods and spending time in nature. Kapha, which is cool and heavy, needs heat, activity and movement.

When you understand your dosha and the intimate relationship between your body and mind, you will experience life differently. It will inspire you to be disciplined to cook, a great act of self-nurturance. You will also desire an experience of silence regularly through meditation and be more inclined to exercise often.

Vedic food is prepared by a happy and conscious cook and is offered to the Divine before it is served to the family. This meal is called "Prasad."

Vedic cooking does not advocate the use of animal protein or even eggs. Ghee, milk and yogurt are considered as gifts from "Kamadhenu" the one who fulfills all desires and wishes. The use of animal flesh is forbidden not only because of the practice of "ahimsa," or non-violence but also as a way to experience our deeper connection to Nature.

Eating "Prasad" is a conscious experience in that we are eating food that was prepared for and offered to the Divine. It is infused with love and higher consciousness. It is understood that food prepared for the Divine is done with a great deal of love and pure feelings. Although Vedic food is delicious, it is not prepared simply for pleasure. Each meal purifies and strengthens our body, mind and hearts. Vedic cooking can be decadent during festivals and celebrations. For everyday cooking, it is simple and based on sound principles of balancing doshas and enhancing digestion and increasing ojas.

Vedic food has a saatvic quality. The three gunas or qualities of Nature are Sattva, Rajas and Tamas. Vedic cooking encourages the use of Saatvic ingredients such as almonds, ghee, rice, mung dal and saffron. Sattvic food creates happiness, gives strength, and calms and purifies the mind. Rajasic foods such as garlic, alcohol and hot spices are considered too stimulating. Tamasic foods such as leftovers and animal flesh are considered too dulling and can cause inertia. Further, leftovers, old and frozen foods are not considered optimal for digestion. Thus it is best to cook a fresh meal each day. Leftovers have very little prana and will not support vitality, radiance or energy. All the recipes in this book will allow you to prepare a fresh meal each day because of its simplicity and ease.

Vedic food also pacifies all three doshas by including six tastes in a meal namely, sweet, salty, pungent, astringent, bitter and sour. One does not have to consume large amounts to satisfy the six tastes.

A bit of lime juice on the greens and lentils is plenty to satisfy sour, and the bitter and astringent come from the greens and lentils respectively. Eating a meal with all six tastes is not only is a pleasurable experience, it also reduces cravings. An example of a typical Vedic meal includes rice with a bit of ghee, lentils or dal, lassi, sautéed zucchini or greens, some ginger and black pepper in the dal and zucchini to satisfy the pungent quality. The salt in the food will satisfy the salty taste.

After eating a Vedic meal, you will experience good energy and will feel blissful and joyful. It purifies the body and mind, preparing us for spiritual awakening. Food is medicine and it supports living our highest Dharma. So, cook and enjoy in good health!

The belly rules the mind
~Spanish Proverb

Staples of a Vedic Kitchen

YOU ARE MORE INCLINED TO COOK IF you have all the necessary ingredients and tools easily available at home. This section is a guide for setting up the basic tools and staples of a vedic kitchen.

TOOLS:
5 cup rice cooker with a stainless steel insert
(Miracle is a good brand)
A fine grater for grating ginger
A good quality chef's knife
A good quality serrated knife
A good quality paring knife
3-5 wooden spoons
A stainless steel soup ladle
A stainless steel spatula
A couple of serving spoons
A salad spinner
Several glass containers in different sizes for
storing dry goods
A 10 inch cast iron skillet
A 3 quart cast iron, clay or stainless steel pot
A couple of 2-4 quart stainless steel pots
A fine mesh strainer
A pair of tongs

GLASS JARS THAT CAN HOLD ABOUT 2-3LBS OF
dry goods are a good investment for your kitchen.
You can easily see how much you have and also having
everything organized creates good energy and
gives you the feeling of abundance.

ALWAYS HAVE ON HAND ABOUT 3 LBS OF
THE FOLLOWING:
White Basmati rice
Brown Basmati rice
Quinoa
French lentils
Mung dal
Red lentils
(Experiment cooking with other lentils such as Beluga,
Green lentils, Urad dal and Chana dal.)
Black beans
Navy beans
Kidney beans
Grapeseed or Safflower oil, and Olive oil

SPICES:
Turmeric
Cumin
Coriander
Fennel
Mustard seeds
Asafetida or Hing (in Hindi)
Cinnamon
Saffron
Clove

FOR SNACKING:
Cashews
Almonds
Dried figs
Raisins
Dates

Kitchen Tantra

How your food is prepared is as important as what food you prepare.

This section gives you some tips and suggestions for making your cooking and dining experience pleasurable.

Cooking is like love. It should be entered into with abandon or not at all.
~Harriet Van Horne

A clean body, a clear mind and a clean kitchen are prerequisites to cooking. Vedic food is always offered to the divine before it is served. Thus a simple prayer silently invoked is a good way to begin cooking.

Cook with reverence because you are taking care of your health and well-being. It is one of the greatest acts of self-nurturance.

Cook in a pleasant environment and enjoy the process with loved ones.

Eat at approximately the same time each day. For optimal digestion, absorption and elimination have breakfast by 8-8:30 a.m, lunch by noon-1p.m and finish dinner by 7p.m.

Indulge in pleasant conversation or enjoy the taste and texture of foods in your mouth in silence.

Eat Slowly and savor te taste and textures of the food

Value the dietary change that is required when seasons change.

Eat the most fresh, organic foods that are available seasonally to experience abundant prana in your body/mind. Make it a habit to shop at farmer's markets.

The best pans to use for cooking are clay, stainless steel or cast iron. Ideally, a gas stove is best. Avoid Teflon and non-stick pans, aluminum, and other coated pans to avoid toxins.

Honor the needs of your body ~ stressful situations require less food intake. Try not to eat heavy foods when you are sad, lonely or upset.

Sip warm water with your meals. Avoid icy, cold drinks in order to maintain strong digestive fire.

Eat foods containing all six tastes – sweet, sour, salty, bitter, astringent and pungent to feel satiated.

Bless your food each time you dine.

After you eat, be sure to remain seated for 10-15 minutes. Too much activity immediately after eating impairs digestion. If you have time, take a brief and leisurely stroll. Napping after meals is a not advisable. A healthy, balanced meal will give you energy, leaves you feeling cheerful and satiated andbalance the doshas

Remember you are what you eat.

Mantras for cooking or to chant before eating:
Om Annapurnaye namaha or:
Om hreem shreem kleem namo bagavatae maheshwari annapurne swaha.

Hrem, shree and kleem are bija mantra (or seed sounds) that invoke the power of Shakti in you, particularly your hands. When you cook you will transmit that power into the food you prepare. *Namo* means to bow down or to honor. Even this brief moment of humility allows us greater receptivity to the Divine. *Bagavatae* means the divine, *Maheshwari* is the wife of Shiva, *Annapurne* is the form of Maheshwari who feeds the universe and Swaha means to offer. The mantra is translated as: "*I honor the goddess, the wife of Shiva who feeds the world. To her, I offer my gratitude for this food.*"

Spices

SPICES NOT ONLY ADD EXOTIC AND AROMATIC flavors to food, they contain tremendous intelligence and medicinal properties. Spices feature strongly in Vedic cooking. They are used in varying proportions according to season and doshic needs. Spices are a quick way of ensuring that all six Ayurvedic tastes—sweet, sour, salty, pungent, bitter and astringent—are included in every meal.

Saffron is the queen of spices and for good reason. It has the highest saatvic vibration of all spices. Saffron is the dried stamens of the crocus flower and the laborious harvesting process is the reason for the high cost of the spice. Black pepper originates from India and is still the king of the spice trade. Cinnamon, cardamom, clove, turmeric, cumin and fennel are commonly used in Vedic cooking.

Cooling spices and herbs include fennel, coriander, mint, turmeric, cilantro, mint and dill.

Pittas tend to do well with small amounts of cumin, ginger, cardamom and sea salt as well. They do best by avoiding cayenne and black pepper.

Vatas and kaphas have a wide range of spices that benefit them. Cumin, black pepper, ginger, garlic, clove, cinnamon, mustard seeds, fenugreek, sea salt, turmeric and saffron are all good for vatas and kaphas. It is best to use chilies and cayenne minimally for vatas.

Always buy organic spices in small quantities. It is best to store spices in a cool and dry place. Glass jars are not effective as exposure to light reduces its potency. Store spices in small stainless steel containers. Dry roast the spices in a skillet on medium heat and allow it to cool completely before grinding in a spice grinder. Roasting the spice releases its powerful aromas and medicinal benefits.

It is important to cook the spices in oil first before adding other ingredients. Always cook the whole spices first before adding the powdered ones to avoid burning the owdered ones.

Warming Spices	Cooling Spices
Cumin	Coriander
Black pepper	Fennel
Garlic	Turmeric
Cayenne	Mint
Chilies	Dill
Clove	Cilantro
Cinnamom	
Fenugreek	
Ginger	
Sea Salt	

Tri-doshic Spice Blend

2 tbsp turmeric
3 tbsp cumin powder
6 tbsp coriander powder
5 tbsp fennel powder
1 tsp black pepper
½ tsp cardamom powder
½ tsp cinnamom powder

Mix the spices well and store in a stainless steel container. Use in soups, dals, beans and vegetables.

Beverages

Lassi

Lassi is a beverage that is served with the meal as a digestive aid. Vedic lassis are much different than the sugar and yogurt laden lassis served in Indian restaurants. Try these lassis for delicious and healthy support for your digestion.

Cumin Lassi

Ingredients:
1½ cups low-fat or non-fat plain yogurt
2½ cups water
½ tsp cumin powder
¾ tsp salt
Optional: 10 mint leaves

Preparation:
Blend all the ingredients together in a blender for 2 minutes and serve at room temperature.

Mint Lassi:

Ingredients:
1½ cups low-fat or non-fat plain yogurt
2½ cups water
½ tsp cumin powder
¾ tsp salt
6-10 mint leaves only (no stems)
6-10 cilantro leaves
A pinch of hing (asafetida)

Preparation:
Blend all the ingredients together in a blender for 2 minutes and serve at room temperature.

Rose Lassi

Ingredients:
1½ cups low-fat or non-fat plain yogurt
2½ cups water
2 tbsp rose water
½ tsp cardamom powder
2 tbsp turbinado sugar

Preparation:
Blend all the ingredients together in a blender for 2 minutes and serve at room temperature.

Mango Milk

Ingredients:
1 ripe mango peeled and all pulp removed
2 cups low fat organic milk
1 tsp cardamom powder
2 tsp rose water (optional)
1 tsp turbinado sugar

Preparation:
Bring the milk to a boil and allow it to cool completely. Place 1 cup of the milk and half the mango pulp and blend till it is smooth. Do the same with the second batch along with the cardamom and sugar. Mix well and serve chilled.

Fresh Almond Milk

Ingredients:
½ cup raw almonds
3 cups water

Preparation:
Soak the almonds in 2 cups of water overnight or in hot water for about 30 minutes. Peel the almonds. Grind it with the 2 cups of water till the almonds are blended finely. You may have to do this in two batches. Place a bowl on the counter and carefully pour the nut milk from the blender into a nutmilk bag or a fine mesh strainer. Discard the almond meal and enjoy the milk in teas, or drinks.

Fig and Date Almond Drink

Ingredients:
3 figs soaked in ½ cup water overnight
5 dates soaked with the figs
1½ cups almond milk (see Fresh Almond Milk recipe)
1 tsp vanilla

Preparation:
Place all the ingredients in a blender and blend for 3 minutes. Serve chilled.

Spiced Milk

Ingredients:
2 cups low fat organic milk
2 cardamom pods
6 almonds soaked in hot water for 30 minutes
5-7 strands of saffron
1/8 tsp cinnamon powder
1 tsp turbinado sugar

Preparation:
Peel the soaked almonds and grind in a blender with ¼ cup of the milk. Break open the cardamom pod and remove the seeds and discard the skin. Then place the ground almonds, cardamom seeds, milk, and the rest of the ingredients in a small pot and bring to a boil. Serve warm with a tiny bit of ghee.

Chutneys

Chutneys are the true appetizers of a Vedic meal. They are eaten in small quantities to ignite the digestive fire. When you invite guests for dinner, prepare several chutneys and let guests choose the ones that pacify their dosha. Chutneys enhance "rasa" and improve digestion.

Ginger Date Chutney

Ingredients:
2 inch piece ginger peeled and chopped coarsely
6 dates pitted and chopped coarsely
½ cup raisins
1 tbsp fennel seeds
½ cup orange juice

Preparation:
Grind all the ingredients coarsely in a food processor till it has the consistency of chutney.

Red Coconut Chutney

Ingredients:
1 cup fresh or unsweetened
dry shredded coconut
¾ tsp salt
1 dry red chili
Juice of ½ lime
½ cup water

Preparation:
Break the red chili in half and remove the seeds. Place all the ingredients in a blender and grind all ingredients till smooth.

Apple Raisin Chutney

Ingredients:
1 tsp oil
1 tsp mustard seeds
½ tsp cinnamon
¼ tsp clove powder
2 tsp grated ginger
½ tsp cumin powder
½ tsp fennel powder
1 tsp coriander powder
⅛ tsp cayenne
3 apples cored peeled and chopped coarsely
½ tsp salt
¼ cup raisins
½ cup water

Preparation:
Heat the oil and add the mustard seeds. Place a lid on it while it pops. Now add all the spices and ginger. Sauté for 30 seconds. Then add the apples, raisins and water. Bring to a boil. Then simmer for about 15-20 minutes or till the apples are tender and soft. Serve at room temperature.

Cashew Cilantro Chutney

Ingredients:
¼ cup cashews
3 tbsp cilantro coarsely chopped
The juice of 1½ - 2 limes
2 tbsp water
½ tsp salt

Preparation:
Soak the cashews for one hour. Drain the water and place all the ingredients in a blender and run till smooth.

Garlic Chutney

Ingredients:
4 tbsp ghee
½ cup peeled garlic cloves
1 cup shredded dry unsweetened coconut
4 tbsp peppercorns
1 tsp coriander seeds
1¼ tsp salt
Juice of 1 lime

Preparation:
Slice the garlic into thin slivers. Heat 2 tbsp of the ghee in a medium skillet and fry the garlic on medium heat for 4-5 minutes or till golden brown. When it cools down, grind the garlic along with the rest of the ingredients in a blender to a fine paste.

Add only a couple of tablespoons of water for ease in grinding. Scrape the sides of the blender as necessary. Heat the remaining ghee and add the ground paste and fry on medium heat for about 12 minutes. This ensures that the garlic is cooked and the moisture evaporates.

Condiments

Raitha

Always prepared with yogurt, they aid in cooling down a spicy meal and like chutneys, are also served in small quantities.

Cucumber and Carrot Raitha

Ingredients:
1 medium sized cucumber
1 medium sized carrot
3 tbsp chopped cilantro
¾ of 32 oz container plain yogurt
¾ tsp salt
½ tsp cumin powder
½ tsp agave nectar

Preparation:
Peel and seed the cucumber and finely chop the cucumber. Grate the carrot. Place all the ingredients in a bowl and mix. Serve at room temperature.

Cucumber Raitha

Ingredients:
1 medium sized cucumber
3 tbsp chopped cilantro
6 mint leaves finely chopped
¾ tsp salt
¾ of 32 oz plain lowfat yogurt

Preparation:
Wash and peel the cucumber. Remove seeds, and chop finely. Mix all the ingredients and serve.

Ghee

Ghee is one of the most ojas rich foods in Ayurveda. It is sweet and cooling, thus a great choice for vata and pitta. Kaphas should use ghee only in moderation.

Ghee

Ingredients:
4 sticks of organic unsalted butter

Preparation:
Place the butter sticks in a medium sized pot and cook on medium high heat cook for 4-5 minutes. When surface is completely covered with foam reduce heat to very low. Cook until a thin crust forms on the surface and the milky white solids fall to the bottom of the pan.

This takes about 15 -20 minutes. When the ghee develops a golden color and stops bubbling and sputtering it is safe assume it is done. Remove from heat, let it cool. Strain with a fine mesh strainer and pour into a jar.

Ghee does not require refrigeration. Be careful to not double dip; and always use a dry spoon to avoid mold.

Stewed Apples and Pears

This is a wonderful and delicious breakfast for improving digestion and elimination. You can use apples alone or pears alone or together as in this recipe. You can also cook figs and raisins soaked overnight with the apples.

Stewed Apples and Pears

Ingredients:
1 apple peeled and chopped coarsely
1 pear peeled and chopped coarsely
3 cloves
1 cup water

Preparation:
Place all the ingredients in a medium sized pot and cover and cook on medium low heat till the fruit is soft – about 20 minutes. If the fruit dries out, add another 1/8 cup of water and cook till it is tender.

Salads and Dressing

A Thing Or Two About Salads:

Ayurveda emphasizes the use of cooked food more than raw foods. Why? Because cooked food is easier to digest. Digesting raw food requires very strong "agni," which most people lack. Having said that, people of all doshas can enjoy salads in moderate amounts as long as the appropriate ingredients are used. Vatas should avoid sprouts, cauliflower, broccoli and beans such as garbanzos but add more steamed vegetables and extra olive oil to their salads. Pittas can use more cucumber, mint and dill. Kaphas can splurge on cooked beans, cruciferous vegetables and a more lemony dressing. In a Vedic meal, there is always something raw, such as the carrot and moong salad in this section. Raw foods are rich in prana but it is best to not serve a main dish. Instead, serve the salad with soup or dal with rice or quinoa.

Tomato-Red Onion Salad with Cilantro

Ingredients:
2 ripe tomatoes cut into 2 inch cubes
1 small red onion thinly sliced
3 tbsp finely chopped cilantro

Optional: 1 medium-sized peeled and de-seeded cucumber cut into 2 inch cubes

Dressing:
2 tbsp olive oil
The juice of 1 lime
3 tbsp plain yogurt
½ tsp agave nectar or turbinado sugar
½ tsp grated ginger – squeeze the juice and add to the dressing.
½ tsp salt
¼ tsp pepper

Preparation:
Place all the chopped vegetables in a bowl. Whisk the dressing ingredients together and drizzle on the salad, mix well and serve.

Carrot and Moong Dal Salad

Ingredients:
3 medium carrots grated
¼ cup moong dal washed and soaked in 1 cup of water for 30 minutes

Dressing:
2 tbsp oil
1 tsp mustard seeds
A pinch of asafetida (hing)
3 tbsp chopped cilantro
Juice of 1 lime
1 tsp salt

Preparation:
Grate the carrots and keep aside. Heat the oil in a small pan and add the mustard seeds. Allow it to pop and turn the heat the off. Then add the hing and sauté for 10 seconds. Re-wash the moong dal and drain all the water and add it along with the lime, salt and the dressing to the grated carrots. Mix well and serve at room temperature.

Lemon Dressing for Green Salads

Ingredients:
The juice of 6 lemons
1 cup extra virgin olive oil
1 tsp salt
1 dash of black pepper
2 tbsp agave nectar

Preparation:
Whisk all the ingredients together and use as needed on salads.

Optional:
1 tbsp finely chopped fresh dill
The zest of 1 lime
1 tbsp finely chopped fresh purple basil

"A salad *freshens* without enfeebling and *fortifies* without irritating."

~Jean-Anthelme Brillat-Savarin (1755-1826)

Cabbage Salad

Ingredients:
1 cup grated cabbage
The juice of ½ lime
¼ cup grated fresh coconut
2 tbsp cilantro
2 tsp oil
1 tsp mustard seeds
A pinch of hing (asafetida)
1 serrano chili slit lengthwise

Preparation:
Mix the grated cabbage, lime juice, cilantro and coconut together in a bowl and set aside. Heat oil in a small pan and add the mustard seeds. Place a lid and allow them to pop. Then add hing and serrano. Stir till the serrano is fried (about 1 minute) and add this to the salad. Mix well and serve at room temperature.

Fresh Raspberry Dressing

Ingredients:
1/2 cup olive oil
1/4 cup lemon juice
½ cup fresh raspberries
1 tsp salt
½ tsp pepper
4 tsp agave nectar or 3 tbsp
   turbinado sugar

Preparation:
 Place all the ingredients in a blender and blend till smooth.

Mooli (Daikon Radish) Raitha

Ingredients:
2/3 cup grated white daikon radish
1 cup plain yogurt
The juice of ½ lime
¼ cup grated fresh coconut
2 tbsp cilantro
2 tsp oil
1 tsp mustard seeds
A pinch of hing (asafetida)
1 serrano chili slit lengthwise

Preparation:
Mix the grated daikon, lime juice, cilantro, yogurt, coconut together in a bowl and set aside. Heat oil in a small pan and add the mustard seeds. Place a lid and allow them to pop. Then add hing and serrano. Stir untill the serrano is fried (about 1 minute) and add this to the salad. Mix well and serve at room temperature.

Salad Rolls with Peanut and Tahini Sauce

Ingredients:
10 large green leaf lettuce
1 medium carrot cut into match sticks
1 small handful of Thai basil
1 block of flavored baked tofu
   cut into slivers
1 handful of cilantro leaves
Optional: cucumber sticks, bean sprouts

For peanut sauce:
1 tsp oil
1 clove of garlic finely chopped
¼ tsp cayenne
¼ cup of water
1 tbsp peanut butter
1 tbsp tahini
2 tsp soy sauce
4 leaves of mint finely chopped

Preparation:
Get all the fillings ready for the rolls. Place one lettuce leaf the stem end closest to you. On that end, place a stick or two of carrots, a piece of the tofu and 2 basil and cilantro leaves. Begin rolling the leaf and as you get to the wider edges of it, tuck it in as you would a burrito. And roll till the end. Place a toothpick to hold the roll together. Build the rest in the same way and place in a container with a tight-fitting lid and cover it.

Now prepare the sauce by heating the oil in a small pot. Add the garlic and sauté for 30 seconds. Now add the cayenne and water and bring to a boil. Once the water boils, add the peanut butter and tahini and whisk gently. Add the soy sauce and whisk till the sauce thickens. If the sauce is too thick, add a few tbsp of water. Add the mint before transferring to the bowl. Serve this sauce at room temperature with the rolls.

Vegetables

If you prepare vegetables using Ayurvedic spices and herbs, they will be delicious and mouth-watering. It is good to include different colored vegetables in your diet to derive different nutrients from them.

Of course, eating seasonally is highly recommended. The best way to eat seasonal vegetables is to shop at farmer's markets. Buy the most fresh, organic produce you can find.

Steamed Asparagus

Ingredients:
2 tsp oil
½ tsp grated ginger
½ tsp turmeric
1 bunch asparagus
½ tsp black pepper
½ tsp salt
2-3 tbsp water

Preparation:
Trim about 2 inches off the ends of the asparagus. Heat the oil and add the ginger and turmeric. Saute for about 30 seconds. Now add the asparagus, salt and pepper and sauté on medium high heat for about 3 minutes. Add the water and place a tight-fitting lid and steam for about 3 minutes. Serve warm.

Sautéed Greens and Cabbage

Ingredients:
2 tbsp olive oil
1 tsp ginger grated
½ tsp turmeric
1 bunch swiss chard
1 small cabbage
1 tbsp coriander powder
1¼ tsp salt
½ tsp black pepper
2 tbsp water

Preparation:
Heat the oil in a wok and sauté the ginger and turmeric for about 45 seconds. Then add all the vegetables and cook on high heat for about 4 minutes. Sprinkle the salt, pepper and coriander powder and stir to coat the vegetables. Add the water and cover with a tight-fitting lid and cook for 5-7 minutes. Serve warm.

Zucchini

Ingredients:
2 tbsp oil
½ tsp cumin powder
1 tsp coriander powder
2 tsp fennel powder
½ tsp turmeric
2-3 medium zucchini cut into one inch cubes
¾ tsp salt
2 tsp chopped cilantro or mint leaves

Preparation:
Heat the oil and add the spices. Sauté it for about 30 seconds. Add the zucchini and salt and stir fry on medium-high heat for about 3 minutes. Then place a lid on the skillet and allow it to steam on low heat for about 5 minutes. Add the cilantro or mint and serve warm.

Yams with Ginger

Ingredients:
2 tbsp oil
2 small yams or 1 medium peeled and chopped into 1 inch cubes
A handful of raisins
½ tsp grated ginger
1 tsp salt
½ tsp pepper
4 tbsp water

Preparation:
Heat the oil and add the yams, raisins, ginger, salt and pepper. Sauté on high heat for 4 minutes. Add the water and cover with a tight-fitting lid. Steam the yams for 6-7 minutes on medium low heat. Serve warm.

Cabbage with Coconut

Ingredients:
2 tbsp oil or ghee
1 tsp mustard seeds
¼ tsp turmeric
2 dry red chilies
1 small cabbage finely shredded
¾ tsp salt
¼ cup shredded unsweetened coconut
¼ cup chopped cilantro

Preparation:
Break the chilies in half and shake out the seeds to discard. Heat the oil or ghee and add the mustard seeds. After they pop, add the turmeric and chilies. Saute for one minute. Then add the cabbage and salt. Sauté the cabbage on high heat for 3-5 mins. Then add 2 tbsp water and cover and steam for about 3-5 minutes. Add the coconut and cilantro and serve warm.

Note: If the cabbage is very tender, cooking time will remain 3-4 minutes. Otherwise, steaming for about 6 minutes should suffice.

Lemony Green Beans

Ingredients:
¾ lb green beans trimmed and cut into 2 inch pieces
3 tbsp oil
2 tsp grated ginger
1 tsp cumin powder
2 tbsp coriander powder
½ tsp turmeric
1 tsp fennel powder
½ tsp black pepper
¾ tsp salt
4 tbsp water
The juice of 1 lime

Preparation:
Heat the oil in a large skillet and add the ginger, cumin, coriander, turmeric, and fennel powder. Sauté for about 45 seconds. Then add the green beans, salt and pepper and stir fry on high heat for 3 minutes. Add the water and place a tight-fitting lid and steam on medium low heat for about 6 minutes. Now add the lime juice and mix well before serving.

Coconut Beets

Ingredients:
2 tsp oil
1 tsp mustard seeds
½ tsp turmeric
2 medium sized beets peeled and cut into ½ inch cubes
1 tsp salt
¾ tsp black pepper
5 tbsp water
¼ cup dry shredded unsweetened coconut
2 tbsp chopped cilantro

Preparation:
Heat the oil in a skillet and add the mustard seeds. Place a lid so the popping mustard seeds do not fly out of the skillet. When the seeds stop popping, add the turmeric and sauté for 30 seconds. Now add the beets, salt and pepper and stir fry on medium high heat for about four minutes. Add 5 tbsp of water and place a tight-fitting lid and steam for about 5 -7 minutes. If the beets dry out, add another 2-3 tbsp of water. Now add the coconut and cilantro and serve warm.

Vegetable Fritters

Ingredients:
1 green pepper seeded and cut into 2 inch strips
1 small potato cut into thin ¼ inch thick slices
2 cups of safflower oil

Coating:
1 cup chickpea flour
½ tsp turmeric
1 tsp salt
2 tbsp chopped cilantro
1 tbsp dried fenugreek leaves
1 tsp fennel powder
½ cup water for mixing and add as needed to have consistency of a slightly runny pancake batter

Heat oil in a large wok. Mix all the ingredients for the coating. Place a small amount of the batter into the oil and if it sizzles and rises to the surface immediately, the oil is ready for frying. Dip the vegetables and carefully place in the hot oil in a single layer without crowding. Fry on medium heat for about 5 minutes on each side. Drain on paper towels and serve immediately.

Alternatives:
Cauliflower, broccoli, individual spinach leaves all make great fritters.

Fritter Alternatives:
Cauliflower, broccoli, individual spinach leaves all make great fritters.

Vegetables

Mixed Vegetables

Ingredients:
3 tbsp olive oil
1 tsp grated ginger
¼ tsp cayenne pepper
½ tsp cinnamon powder
1 tsp cumin powder
½ tsp turmeric
1 small eggplant peeled and cut
　into one inch pieces
1 red pepper seeded and cut into
　one inch pieces
1 yellow pepper seeded cut into
　one inch pieces
1 zucchini cut into one inch cubes
1 broccoli crown cut into florets
1 ½ tsp salt
2 tbsp coriander powder

Preparation:
Heat the oil in a wok or large skillet.
Add the ginger, cayenne, cinnamon,
cumin and turmeric. Sauté for 30 seconds and add all the vegetables and salt.
Stir fry on medium high heat for 5-6
minutes. Then add ⅛ cup of water
and place a tight-fitting lid and turn
the heat down to medium. Allow it to
steam for about 5 -7 minutes. Now add
the coriander powder and mix well and
cook for another 2 minutes.
Serve warm.

Savory Corn Fritters

Ingredients:
1 ear of corn, de-husked
1 medium onion thinly sliced
1 clove of garlic finely chopped
½ bunch cilantro finely chopped
½ tsp turmeric
1 tsp salt
½ - ¾ cup of chickpea flour
1 tsp fennel powder
¼ tsp cayenne powder
A sprinkling of water if necessary
2 cups of safflower oil for frying

Preparation:
With a sharp knife, slice the corn from
the ear into a large bowl. Add the onion,
garlic, cilantro, turmeric, salt, chickpea
flour, fennel, and cayenne and mix well.

If the dough is very dry, sprinkle a few
teaspoons of water and let it sit for 10
minutes. Then heat the oil in a medium-
sized wok and re-mix the dough. To test
the oil, carefully drop a tiny bit of the
dough into the oil. If the dough sizzles
and rises to the surface immediately, the
oil is ready. Add 1 tsp of the dough at a
time into the oil.

Do not crowd the wok or else the oil will
cool down. This means the fritters will
absorb much oil. Fry on one side for 2-3
minutes or till golden brown and then
turn the fritters over and fry on the other
side for another 2 minutes or so. Drain
on paper towels and serve immediately
with any of the chutneys from the chutney section of this book. ·

Note: It is best not to re-use this oil.
Find someone in your area that recycles
cooking oil instead of discarding it.

Roasted Vegetables with Tahini Sauce

Ingredients
1 small cauliflower cut into
　medium florets
1 yam peeled and cut into 1 inch
　thick strips
2 medium carrots cut into 1 inch
　thick strips
1 zucchini cut into 2 inch strips
2 tbsp oil
1 tsp salt
¼ tsp black pepper
½ tsp turmeric
½ tsp cinnamon powder
½ tsp cumin powder
1 tsp coriander powder

For dipping sauce:
2 tbsp raw tahini
3 tbsp plain yogurt
Juice of 1 lime
3-5 tbsp water
½ tsp salt

Preparation:
Place the oven setting on broil. Meanwhile, place all the chopped vegetables
in a mixing bowl and drizzle the oil, salt
and pepper. Mix it with your hands to
combine well. Place on a cookie sheet
in a single layer and roast for about 5
minutes. Turn over and roast for another
5 minutes. Meanwhile, in a small bowl,
whisk the dipping sauce ingredients together. Serve with the roasted vegetables.

Roasted Potatoes with Broccolini

Ingredients:
2 medium potatoes
2 tbsp safflower or olive oil
½ tsp cumin powder
½ tsp fennel powder
1 tsp coriander powder
½ tsp turmeric powder
½ tsp pepper
1 tsp salt
Marinade for broccolini:
2 small bunches broccolini
½ tsp pepper
½ tsp salt
2 tsp safflower or olive oil
1 tbsp lime juice

Preparation:
Pre-heat oven to 475 degrees. Wash the potatoes and cut them into 2 inch cubes. Place the potatoes on a cookie sheet and drizzle the oil and spices and mix well with your hands. Roast for 25-35 minutes turning once during roasting. In the meanwhile, wash and trim the ends of the broccolini. Chop them into medium sized florets and drizzle with oil, salt and pepper. Place the marinaded broccolini on another cookie sheet and place it in the oven for 10 minutes. You can place the broccolini in the oven 20 minutes after the potatoes so that both the vegetables are roasted around the same time. When the broccolini is cooked, drizzle the lime juice over it. Place in a serving bowl and add the potatoes. Mix gently. Serve warm.

Vegetables with Tofu

Ingredients:
2 tbsp olive oil
1 clove garlic chopped finely
1 tsp grated ginger
1 cup chopped broccoli
1 medium carrot sliced thinly
2 yellow squash cut into one inch cubes
1 high-protein organic extra firm tofu chopped into one inch cubes
¼ cup reduced sodium soy sauce
½ tsp black pepper
2 tbsp chopped chives for garnish

Preparation:
Heat the oil. Add the ginger and garlic. Sauté on medium heat for 45 seconds. Now add the tofu and stir fry on high for 4-5 minutes. Then add the vegetables and also stir fry on high heat for 3 minutes. Add the soy sauce and pepper. Mix well and cover with a tight-fitting lid and steam for another 4 minutes. Sprinkle on the chives and serve warm.

Gingered Greens with Moong Dal

Ingredients:
2 tbsp oil or ghee
1 tsp mustard seeds
¼ tsp turmeric
1 tbsp moong dal (also spelled as mung dal)
1 large bunch red chard chopped (discard the stems)
¾ tsp salt
¼ cup shredded fresh or dry unsweetened coconut

Preparation:
Soak the moong dal in ½ cup water for 15 minutes. Heat the oil or ghee and add the mustard seeds. Place a lid and once the seeds stop popping, add the moong dal and turmeric and sauté for 1 minute. Then add the red chard and salt and sauté on high heat for 3 minutes. Place a lid on it and steam for about 5 minutes. Then add the coconut and mix well. Serve warm.

Vegetables

Paneer with Mixed Vegetables

Ingredients:
For vegetables:
3 tbsp oil
1 tsp grated ginger
½ tsp turmeric
1 tsp cumin powder
2 tsp fennel powder
1 cup chopped cauliflower
1 cup thinly sliced carrots
1½ cups green beans cut
   into 1 inch pieces
1 cup frozen peas
2 tbsp coriander powder
¼ tsp cayenne
2 tsp salt
½ cup water
¼ cup slivered almonds ground
   into a fine powder
1 cup cubed paneer (see folowing
   recipe for paneer instructions).

Preparation:
Heat the oil and add the ginger and sauté for about 30 seconds. Then add the turmeric and cumin and sauté briefly. Then add all the vegetables and stir fry on high heat. Add the coriander, salt and cayenne. Stir fry for another 2-3 minutes. Add the water and the ground almonds and mix well. Place a lid and allow the vegetables to steam. When the vegetables are about ¾ of the way done, add the paneer and simmer for another 3 minutes.

Paneer Masala

Ingredients:
For the Masala:
3 tbsp oil
1 small onion finely chopped
1 tsp finely chopped garlic
1 tsp grated ginger
½ tsp turmeric
1 tsp cumin powder
2 tsp coriander powder
¼ tsp cinnamon
¼ tsp clove powder
3 large tomatoes finely chopped
¼ tsp cayenne powder
½ tsp sugar
1½ tsp salt
½ cup water
½ cup paneer cubes
4 tbsp finely chopped cilantro

Paneer:
½ gallon organic whole milk
Juice of 1.5 limes

Preparation:
For the paneer, bring the milk to a boil in a medium-sized pot and slowly add the lime juice while stirring constantly. After the whey and curd separate, strain in a colander layered with cheese cloth and place something heavy, such as a cast-iron skillet and allow it to compact.

Leave it like this for about 25 minutes. Remove the cheese cloth and cut into half inch cubes. In the meanwhile, heat the oil in a large pot and add the on-ion, ginger and garlic. Sauté on medium heat for 6-8 minutes or till the onions are soft. Now add all the spice powders except cayenne and sauté for about 45 seconds.

Then add the tomatoes and bring to a boil. Simmer for about 15 minutes till the tomatoes are soft. Add the sugar, salt and cayenne and add the paneer and mix gently. Simmer for another 4 minutes. Just before serving add the cilantro.

Asparagus with Yams

Ingredients:
2 tsp oil or ghee
½ tsp cumin powder
½ tsp turmeric
1 tsp coriander powder
1 yam peeled and chopped into
   one inch cubes
1 bunch asparagus ends trimmed
   and chopped into one inch pieces
1¼ tsp salt
¼ tsp black pepper
1/8 cup of water

Preparation:
Heat the oil or ghee in a skillet. Add the spices and sauté for about 30-40 seconds. Add the yam and stir fry on medium high heat for about 4 minutes. Then add the asparagus, salt and pepper and sauté for 2-3 minutes. Add the water and place a tight-fitting lid and steam for about 4 -5 minutes. Serve warm.

Sauteed Greens

Ingredients:
2 tsp ghee or oil
½ tsp turmeric
1 bunch Swiss chard
½ tsp salt
¼ tsp black pepper
The juice of ½ lime

Preparation:
Wash the swiss chard well to ensure that all the sand a grit is drained off. Chop coarsely and keep aside. Heat the ghee in a large skillet and add the turmeric and saute for 30 seconds. Add the swiss chard, salt and pepper. Stir fry on high heat for about 3 minutes. Add 4 tbsp of water and place a tight-fitting lid and steam for about 5 minutes. Serve warm.

Spinach Bhaji

Ingredients:
2 tbsp oil
1tsp cumin seeds
1 tsp methi (fenugreek) seeds
½ tsp turmeric
A pinch of hing (asafetida)
2 medium tomatoes finely chopped
2 bunches spinach washed and
    finely chopped
¼ tsp cayenne
1¼ tsp salt
1 tbsp coriander powder

Preparation:
Heat oil and add the cumin and methi seeds. After they sizzle for 30 seconds, add the hing and turmeric. Saute for about 30 seconds. Now add the tomatoes and cook on medium heat it is soft and well-cooked. Add the chopped spinach, cayenne, salt and coriander powder and cook only until the spinach wilts. Serve warm.

Cabbage with Fenugreek

Ingredients:
2 tsp ghee
½ tsp cumin powder
½ tsp turmeric
1 tbsp coriander powder
1 small cabbage shredded coarsely
1 bunch fenugreek
1 tsp salt
½ tsp pepper

Preparation:
Wash the fenugreek and trim the bottom 3 inches off and discard. Finely chop the rest of the leaves and tender stems. Heat the ghee in a wok or skillet. Add the spice powders and sauté for about 30 seconds. Add the fenugreek leaves and stir fry on medium heat for about 3 minutes. Then add the cabbage, salt and pepper and stir fry on high heat for about 4 minutes. Place a tight-fitting lid and steam for about 4 minutes. Serve warm.

Warming Squash Soup

Ingredients:
2 tbsp oil or 2 tbsp ghee
½ cup thinly sliced leeks
1 tsp grated ginger
1 tsp finely chopped garlic
1 tsp turmeric
1½tsp cumin powder
1 tbsp fennel powder
1 tbsp coriander
½ tsp cayenne
½ tsp fresh rosemary finely chopped
½ tsp fresh oregano finely chopped
1 cup finely chopped tomatoes
1 medium yam peeled and cut
    into 1 inch cubes
1 cup chopped butternut squash (one
inch cubes)
1½ tsp salt
1½ cups water

Preparation:
Heat the ghee or oil in a large pot and add the leeks, ginger and garlic and sauté on medium heat for about 5 minutes. Now add the spices along with rosemary and oregano. Sauté for another 2 minutes. Then add the tomatoes and cook on medium heat for about 7 minutes or till the tomatoes are soft.

Now add the yam, butternut squash and salt and bring to a boil. Cover and simmer on medium heat for 8-12 minutes or till the vegetables are tender. Serve warm.

Vegetables

Mixed Vegetable Curry with Coconut

Ingredients:
15 green beans trimmed and cut
    into 2 inch pieces
1 medium carrot thinly sliced
1 chayote squash peeled and cored and
cut into 2 inch cubes (substitute zucchini, if chayote is not available)
1 cup frozen green peas
1½ tsp salt
¼ cup water
¾ cup of water
Juice of ½ lime

Grind together:
¾ cup shredded coconut
1 tsp cumin seeds
1 serrano
5 tsp chopped cilantro
1 one inch piece fresh ginger
¼ cup water

Preparation:
Place the water and the vegetables along
with the salt in a medium pot and bring
to a boil. Simmer gently for about 5
minutes. In the meanwhile, grind the
coconut with spices and add to the
vegetables and simmer for another 5
minutes. Add the lime just before
serving.

Mixed Vegetable Curry II

Ingredients:
1 small yam peeled and chopped into
   1- inch cubes
1 cup cubed butternut squash
1 green bell pepper cut into 1 inch cubes
1 cup coarsely chopped cabbage
½ tsp salt
¾ cup of water

Roast the following in 1 tsp oil
on medium heat till fragrant
(about 3-4 minutes):
1 tsp fenugreek (methi) seeds
1 tsp cumin seeds
2 red chilies broken in half
   and seeds discarded
1 one-inch piece cinnamon stick
4 black peppercorns

For coconut sauce:
½ tsp turmeric
¾ cup shredded coconut
1/3 cup of water or a bit more for
   ease in grinding
2-3 tbsp lime juice
2 tbsp turbinado sugar

Preparation:
Place the vegetables, salt and water in
a medium sized pot and bring to a boil.
Simmer the vegetables gently for about
5 minutes. Place the coconut paste
ingredients along with the roasted spices
in a blender and grind to a smooth
paste. Add the coconut mix to the
vegetables and bring to a gentle boil.
Simmer for about 5 minutes.
Serve warm.

Baby Bok Choy with Cashews

Ingredients:
2 tbsp oil
1 small clove of garlic chopped finely
½ tsp turmeric
10 whole cashews
6 baby bok choy
2 tsp soy sauce
½ tsp black pepper

Preparation:
Soak the bok choy in a bowl of water to
remove the sand and dirt. Drain and
cut the bok choy in half lengthwise.
Heat the oil in a skillet and add the
chopped garlic and turmeric.
Cook for about 45 seconds.

Now add the cashews and cook for
about 1 minute. Now add the chopped
bok choy, soy sauce and black pepper
and cook on medium high heat for
about 3 minutes. Place a tight-fitting
lid and steam for about 3 minutes.
Serve warm.

Cabbage with Kale

Ingredients:
2 tbsp oil
1 tsp grated ginger
1 tsp fennel seeds
½ tsp turmeric
1½ cups coarsely chopped cabbage
1½ cups coarsely chopped kale
1 tsp salt
The juice of ½ lime

Preparation:
Heat oil and add the ginger and fennel seeds. Saute for about 1 minute. Now add the turmeric and cook for about 45 seconds. Now add the cabbage and kale and turn up the heat. Add the salt and 4 tbsp water and cover with a tight-fitting lid and steam for about 6 minutes. Now add the lime juice and serve warm.

Chard with Carrots

Ingredients:
2 tbsp oil
1 tsp grated ginger
1 tbsp white sesame seeds
½ tsp turmeric
1 medium carrot thinly sliced
2 cups swiss chard coarsely chopped
¼ tsp cayenne
1 tsp salt

Preparation:
Heat the oil and add the ginger and sesame seeds. Saute for about 1 minute. Now add the turmeric and cook for 45 seconds.

Now add the carrots and stir-fry on medium heat for 4 minutes. Now add the chard and salt and stir fry for about 3-4 minutes. Add 4 tbsp of water and cover with a tight-fitting lid and steam for about 5 minutes. Serve warm.

Carrots with Cinnamon

Ingredients:

1 tbsp ghee
½ tsp cinnamon
¼ tsp clove powder
A pinch of nutmeg
3 medium carrots thinly sliced
1tsp salt
1 tsp turbinado sugar
5-6 tbsp of water

Preparation:
Heat the ghee in a skillet and add the cinnamon, clove and nutmeg. Cook it on medium heat for about 45 seconds. Now add the carrots and mix well to coat the carrots with the spices. Now add the salt, sugar and water and cook on high heat for 3 minutes. Place a tight-fitting lid and steam the carrots for 6-8 minutes Serve warm.

Satya's   Potato Sabzi

Ingredients:
2 tbsp oil
1 tsp cumin seeds
A pinch of hing (asafetida)
½ tsp turmeric
2 medium tomatoes finely chopped
2 tsp coriander powder
2 medium sized russet potatoes peeled and cut into 1 inch cubes
¼ tsp cayenne
1½ tsp salt
¼ cup water

Preparation:
Heat the oil in a medium sized pot and add the cumin seeds. Allow them to sizzle or about 40 seconds. Now add the hing and turmeric and cook or about 30 seconds. Add the tomatoes and coriander and cook on medium heat till the tomatoes are soft and well-cooked.

Now add the potatoes, cayenne, salt and water and bring to a boil. Place a tight-fitting lid and turn down the heat to low and cook for about 10 minutes or till the potatoes are tender. Serve warm.

Vegetables

Okra

Ingredients:
2 tbsp oil
1 lb tender okra
1 tsp cumin seeds
½ tsp turmeric
¼ tsp cayenne
1 tbsp coriander powder
¾ tsp salt

Preparation:
Wash and completely dry the okra with a dishcloth. Then trim off the ends and chop them into thin rounds. Heat the oil a skillet and add the cumin seeds. Next add the turmeric, coriander and cayenne and cook for about 30 seconds. Add the okra and sauté on medium high heat for about 5 minutes. Now turn the heat down to medium low and cook, stirring occasionally for another 12 minutes. When the okra is no longer slimy, add the salt and cook for another 3 minutes. Serve warm.

Opo Squash

Ingredients:
2 tbsp oil
1 tsp cumin seeds
½ tsp turmeric
½ tsp black pepper
1 tsp coriander powder
1 medium opo squash peeled and
   cut into 1 inch cubes
¾ tsp salt

Preparation:
Heat the oil in a skillet and add the cumin seeds. Allow it to sizzle for 45 seconds. Now add the turmeric, black pepper and coriander powder and sauté for about 30 seconds. Add the opo squash and salt and cook on high heat for about 2 minutes. Place a tight-fitting lid and cook on medium low heat for about 6 minutes. Serve warm.

Raw spinach Pesto with Nuts and Herbs

Ingredients:
1 small bag of baby spinach
1 clove of garlic
The juice of 1 lemon
¼ cup packed basil leaves
¼ cup extra virgin olive oil
12 blanched almonds or walnuts
½ tsp salt
½ black pepper
½ cup parmesan cheese

Preparation:
Place all the pesto ingredients in a food processor except the olive oil. Turn it on and drizzle the oil slowly till you have the consistency of pesto. Use with pasta or as a spread for sandwiches.

Hoopla Lumpia

Ingredients:
2 tbsp oil
1 small onion sliced
1 clove of garlic finely chopped
2 medium-sized carrots julienned
15 green beans julienned
1 cup finely shredded cabbage
1 tsp Chinese 5 spice powder
2 tbsp turbinado sugar
1 cup bean sprouts
2 tbsp soy sauce
10 spring roll wrappers
Oil for brushing
3 tbsp black sesame seeds

Preparation:
Saute the onions and garlic in the oil until the onions are soft. Add carrots, green beans and cabbage and cook for 4-5 minutes. Now add the Chinese 5 spice powder, turbinado sugar, bean sprouts and soy sauce and bean sprouts and cook for 2 minutes. Set aside to cool. Heat the oven to 350 degrees.

Separate the spring roll wrappers. Spoon about 1 tbsp of the filling near the center of the wrapper. Turn the bottom edge over to cover the filling, and then fold in the left and right sides. Roll the wrapper up almost to the top then brush the top edge with water and seal. Repeat this procedure with the remaining wrappers and filling. Brush each hoopla spring roll with oil and sprinkle the sesame seeds on top and place in a sheet pan and bake for 20 minutes or till golden brown. Serve immediately.

Hoopla Spinach

Ingredients:
2 tbsp oil
1 medium onion thinly sliced
4 bunches of spinach
3 tbsp olive oil
2 cloves of garlic finely chopped
½ tsp coriander powder
1 tsp salt
½ tsp pepper
The juice of 2 lemons

Preparation:
Heat the 2 tbsp oil and cook the onion on medium heat till brown. Stir often. Keep aside. Wash and drain the spinach. Place it in a large pot with 5 tbsp of water. Turn the heat to high and steam the spinach just until it wilts. This will be very quick. Drain and cool and squeeze out all the water from the spinach with your hands.

Chop it coarsely and keep aside. Now heat the 3 tbsp of olive oil and add the garlic and coriander. Let it cook for 1 minute. Mix the garlic with the spinach along with the salt, pepper and lemon juice. Place in a bowl and garnish with the onions. Serve immediately.

Vegetables in Coconut Milk

Ingredients:
1 medium carrot cut into 2 inch sticks
1 chayote squash peeled and cut into 2 inch sticks
10 green beans stringed and cut into 2 inch pieces
1 small yam peeled and cut into 2 inch sticks
½ cup of water
1 tsp turmeric
1¼ tsp salt
1 cup grated fresh coconut or 1 cup dry unsweetened shredded coconut
1 jalapeno with seeds and membranes removed
3 tbsp plain yogurt
2 tbsp coconut oil
10 fresh curry leaves

Preparation:
Place all the vegetables, water and salt and bring to a boil. Simmer for 4 minutes and turn off the heat. In the meanwhile, grind the coconut with jalapeno, turmeric, using ¼ cup of water to a fine paste. Use only a small amount of extra water for ease in grinding. Add the coconut mixture to the cooked vegetables and cook on low heat. Now add the yogurt and continue to cook on low heat. Heat the coconut oil in a small pan and add the curry leaves. Fry for about 1 minute and add to the vegetables. Simmer for another 2-3 minutes. If re-heating later, do so on low heat so the yogurt and coconut sauce does not curdle.

Cauliflower with coconut

Ingredients:
2 tbsp coconut oil
2 dry red chilies, broken in half and seeds discarded
1 tbsp coriander seeds
1 medium cauliflower cut into small florets
1 cup fresh or dry unsweetened dry shredded coconut
1 tbsp lemon juice
1 small onion chopped finely
½ tsp turmeric
1½ tsp salt

Preparation:
Heat 1 tsp of the oil and roast the chilies and coriander seeds for 3-4 minutes. Keep aside to cool. Now add the chilies and coriander to the coconut, lemon juice along with ¼ cup of water and grind to a paste. If you need to add more water add a tiny bit at a time.

The paste should be thick when it is ground up. Heat the rest of the oil in a skillet and cook the onions and turmeric on medium heat till transparent. Add the cauliflower and cook on medium heat for about 4 minutes. Add the coconut paste, mix well and cook on low for about 5 minutes. If the heat is too high, the coconut paste will curdle. Serve warm.

Grains

Ayurveda states that grains support the growth of muscle tissue and bone and provide physical strength and endurance. Grains are useful to vegetarians because they help in creating whole proteins when combined with legumes and beans ~ rice and lentils are a great combination. Grains such as brown and white basmati rice are easily available and are easy to cook. Quinoa, polenta and spelt are other easy to use grains. Ayurveda recommends having grains at each meal to provide adequate energy for the body and for satisfying the taste of sweetness.

Basmati Rice with Whole Spices and Paneer

Ingredients:
2 tbsp oil or ghee
1 bay leaf
1 tsp cumin seeds
1 cinnamon stick
2 cardamom pods
5-7 strands of saffron
1 cup rice
2 cups water
1 tsp salt

Paneer:
½ gallon organic whole milk
Juice of 1½ limes
2 tsp ghee
¼ tsp turmeric
½ tsp ginger
½ tsp salt

Preparation:
Bring the milk to a boil in a medium-sized pot and slowly add the lime juice while stirring constantly. After the whey and curd separate, strain with a fine mesh strainer or cheese cloth in a colander and place something heavy, such as a cast-iron skillet and allow it to compact. Leave it like this for about 25 minutes. Then with a sharp knife, cut the paneer into small cubes. Heat ghee and add the turmeric. Saute briefly and then add the paneer and fry on medium heat for about 5-7 minutes, carefully turning the paneer occasionally. Keep aside.

Meanwhile, wash the rice in three changes of water. Drain completely. In a medium-sized pot, heat the oil and add the whole spices. Sauté gently for 1 minute and then add the washed and drained rice. Sauté for 3 minutes. Add the water and bring to a boil. Place the lid on it and cook on low heat for 15 mins. Let the rice sit for five minutes. Add the fried paneer to the cooked rice. Mix gently and serve warm.

Basic Basmati Rice with Ghee

Ingredients:
1 cup white basmati rice
2 cups of water
1 tbsp ghee
1 bay leaf
½ tsp cumin seeds
½ tsp salt

Preparation:
Wash the rice in three changes of water and drain completely. Melt the ghee in a medium sized pot and add the bay leaf and cumin seeds. Saute for about 45 seconds. Add the well-drained rice and salt and stir fry for about 2-3 minutes. Now add the 2 cups of water and bring to a rapid boil. Cover with a tight-fitting lid and cook on low heat for 15 minutes. Serve warm.

Dill Rice with Carrots

Ingredients:
2 tbsp olive oil or ghee
1 cup brown rice
1 tsp salt
½ tsp pepper
2 cups water
½ tsp turmeric
1 tsp cumin powder
1 large bunch dill
1 medium carrot thinly sliced

Preparation:
Heat one tbsp of oil or ghee and sauté the brown rice for about 3-4 minutes. Then add the water and bring to a boil. Place a tight-fitting lid and cook on low for about 40 minutes. Remove the stems from the dill and chop finely. Add the remaining one tbsp of oil to a skillet, sauté the turmeric and cumin for about 30 seconds. Now add the carrot and dill and sauté for about 5 minutes. Add the vegetables to the rice and mix well. Serve warm.

Mint-cilantro Rice with Cashews and Vegetables

Ingredients:

1 cup Basmati rice

2 cups water

¾ tsp salt

3 tbsp oil

1 bay leaf

1 star anise

1 cinnamon stick

2 cloves

1 tsp cumin seeds

1 cardamom pod

½ small onion thinly sliced

½ tsp turmeric

1 clove garlic finely chopped

½ inch piece of ginger grated

10 whole cashews

15 green beans trimmed and cut
into 1 inch pieces

1 medium carrot thinly sliced

½ small cauliflower cut into florets

½ tsp salt

In a blender grind finely:

1 medium bunch cilantro

15 mint leaves

½ tsp black pepper

¼ cup of water

Preparation:

Wash the rice in three changes of water. Drain completely. In a medium-sized pot, add the rice and measured water and salt and bring to a boil. Cover with a tight-fitting lid and cook on low heat for 15 minutes. Turn the heat off and let it to sit for 5 minutes before opening. In the meanwhile, in a large skillet, heat the oil and add the whole spices. Sauté for 45 seconds then add the onion, turmeric, ginger and garlic. Stir-fry on medium heat for about 6 minutes.

Then add the cashews and cook for another 2 minutes. Now add the vegetables and salt turn the heat up to high and stir fry for 4 minutes. Add the ground cilantro-mint paste and cook on high heat till all the water has evaporated. Mix with the cooked rice and serve warm.

Spelt Flatbread with Ghee

Ingredients:

1 cup organic spelt flour

¼ cup water

½ tsp salt

1 tbsp oil

Ghee for smearing

Preparation:

Place the flour and salt in a mixing bowl and add the water slowly. Mix with your hands till dough is formed. Once the dough ball comes together, add the oil and knead it for about 4 minutes. Cover the bowl and let it rest for 20 minutes. Heat a cast iron skillet. In the meanwhile, make a 2 inch ball of the dough and roll it out into a thin and even disk about 4-5 inches in diameter. Cook on medium high till it begins to puff up gently. Turn over and cook on the other side. Place the bread in a container with a lid and drizzle about one tsp of ghee on the flatbread. Keep it covered so they remain soft. Continue with the dough till all breads are cooked. Yield : 6

Spiced Quinoa

Ingredients:

1 cup quinoa

2 cups of water

2 tbsp oil

1 tsp grated ginger

½ tsp cumin powder

1 tbsp coriander powder

½ tsp turmeric

¼ tsp cinnamon powder

One handful of cashews

One handful of raisins

¾ tsp salt

The juice of one lime

Preparation:

Soak the quinoa in 3 cups of water for 30 minutes. Rinse and wash again and drain completely. Add the water to the washed quinoa and bring to a boil. Cover with a tight-fitting lid and cook on low for 20 minutes. In the meantime, heat the oil and add the ginger, spice powders, cashews, and raisins. Saute for 45 seconds. When the quinoa is cooked, mix in the spices and lime juice. Serve warm.

Grains

Rice with Lentils

Ingredients:
½ cup brown rice
½ cup brown, green or French lentils
2½ cups of water
2 cups of baby spinach leaves

For the spice mix:
2 tbsp olive oil
½ tsp ginger
½ tsp turmeric
1 tsp fennel powder
2 tsp coriander powder
½ tsp cumin powder
1½ tsp salt
½ tsp black pepper

Preparation:
Soak the lentils for 3 hours. Wash the lentils in two changes of water and drain completely. Wash the rice and drain completely. In a medium sized pot, heat the oil, and add the ginger and spices and sauté for about 45 seconds. Now add the rice and lentils and sauté for about 2 minutes. Add the water, salt and pepper and bring to a boil. Place a tight-fitting lid and cover and cook on low heat for about 35 minutes. Add ½ cup of baby spinach leaves per person and serve with a tsp of ghee in each bowl.

Un-Fried Rice

Ingredients:
1 cup white Basmati rice
2 cups water
1 tsp salt
2 tbsp oil
1 tsp grated ginger
1 carrot thinly sliced
15-20 green beans chopped into
    one inch pieces
½ of small cabbage thinly shredded
(optional: 10 asparagus stalks, ½
    red pepper)
½ tsp salt
1 tsp pepper
2 stalks green onions thinly sliced

Preparation:
Wash the rice in three changes of water. Drain completely. Now add two cups of water and one tsp salt and bring to a boil. Place a tight-fitting lid and cook on low for 15 minutes. In the meanwhile, heat the oil in a wok or large skillet. Add all the vegetables and ginger and stir fry on high heat for 6-8 minutes. Add salt and pepper. When the rice has cooled, add it to the cooked veggies and stir fry for 2-3 minutes. Add the green onions and serve warm.

Khicidi

Ingredients:
¾ cup white Basmati rice
¼ cup moong dal
5 cups water
1 tsp salt

For the spice mix:
3 tbsp oil or 3 tbsp ghee
¾ tsp cumin powder
¼ tsp turmeric
½ tsp black pepper powder
½ tsp fennel powder
¼ tsp cinnamon powder
½ tsp grated ginger
2 tsp chopped cilantro

Preparation:
Soak the dal for one hour. Wash and drain completely. Wash the rice in three changes of water. Drain completely. Add the measured water and salt and bring to a boil. Once it comes to a rolling boil, place a tight-fitting lid and cook on low heat for 35 minutes. In the meanwhile, heat the oil or ghee in a small pot and add all the spices. Sauté for about 45 seconds and then add the ginger. Sauté for about a minute and add the spice mix to the cooked rice and dal mix. Mix well and garnish with the chopped cilantro. Serve immediately with one teaspoon of ghee for each bowl of khicidi.

Jeweled Rice

Ingredients:

3 tbsp ghee
3 bay leaves
4 whole cardamom pods
½ tsp turmeric
½ tsp cinnamon powder
A pinch of nutmeg
¼ tsp clove powder
A small handful of dried cranberries
A small handful of raisins
4 dried apricots chopped coarsely
A small handful of pistachios
A small handful of cashews
1 ½ cups of white basmati rice
2 ¾ cups of water
4 tbsp turbinado sugar
1 tsp salt
10-14 strands of saffron

Preparation:

Wash the rice in three changes of water and drain completely. Keep aside. Heat the ghee in a medium sized pot and add the bay leaves and cardamom pods. Cook for about 45 seconds. Now add the turmeric, cinnamon, nutmeg and clove powders and cook for about 30 seconds. Now add the cranberries, raisins, apricots, pistachios and cashews and stir fry for about 1 minute. Now add the washed rice and stir fry on medium heat for about 3 minutes. Add the water, sugar, salt and saffron and bring to a rapid boil. Cover with a tight-fitting lid and cook on low heat for 15 minutes. Let it stand for 5 minutes before opening. Serve warm.

Polenta with Sautéed Spinach and Goat Cheese

Ingredients:

1 tube of organic polenta
2 bags of baby spinach
4 tbsp oil
2 cloves of garlic finely chopped
1 tsp salt
Generous grinding of pepper
4 oz. package of goat cheese

Preparation:

Pre-heat oven to 300°. Cut the ends of the polenta package and discard, and place it on a cutting board. Using a sharp knife cut the polenta into 1 inch thick rounds. Heat ½ tbsp oil in a skillet and place the polenta in the pan in a single layer. Allow it to brown gently for about 4 minutes. Turn it over and cook for 3 minutes. Place the cooked polenta on a platter and keep warm in the oven. Meanwhile, heat 1 tbsp of oil and add the garlic and sauté for 45 seconds. Then add the spinach and quickly saute it with salt and pepper. Place a tablespoon of the spinach on each polenta round and then top it with a dollop of goat cheese. Serve warm.

Pasta with and Basil

Ingredients:

½ package of whole wheat pasta or rice pasta
1 tbsp olive oil
1 clove garlic finely chopped
2 medium zucchini cut lengthwise in half and then chopped into half moons
¼ cup sun-dried tomatoes (in oil)
½ cup pine nuts toasted
1 tsp salt
Pepper to taste
4 tbsp chopped basil
½ cup crumbled goat cheese

Preparation:

Boil water in a medium sized pot and cook the pasta according to directions on the package. Place the pine nuts in a small skillet and toast on medium low heat for about 4 minutes. Keep aside. Heat the oil in a skillet and add the garlic. Sauté for about 30 seconds. Then add the zucchini and ½ tsp salt. Stir-fry on medium high heat for about 4 minutes. Add the sun-dried tomatoes and pepper and heat through. Add all the vegetables to the cooked pasta along with pine nuts, basil and mix well. Top with goat cheese and serve immediately.

Grains

"Sweeten Your Day" Breakfast Quinoa

Ingredients:
2 tbsp raisins
5 raw almonds
1 fig
1 cup quinoa
½ apple peeled and cut into small cubes
1¾ cups water
2 tbsp ghee
A few strands of saffron
1 star anise
½ tsp cardamom powder
½ tsp cinnamon
⅛ tsp clove powder
3 tbsp agave
A pinch of salt

Preparation:
Soak the almonds, raisins and fig in ½ cup of water overnight. Soak the quinoa in 3 cups of water for 30 minutes. Rinse and wash again and drain completely in a fine mesh strainer. In a medium-sized pot, heat the ghee on medium heat and add the star anise. Sauté for about 30 seconds.

Add the drained quinoa, cubed apple, saffron and spice powders and cook, stirring often for about three to four minutes. Remove the skin from the almonds and chop coarsely. Chop the fig coarsely and add it along with the nuts, and raisins to the quinoa. Sauté for another two to three minutes.

Now add the water, salt and agave and bring to a boil. Place a tight-fitting lid on the pot and cook on low for 18-20 minutes. If you prefer a creamier texture, add an extra ½ cup of water or fresh almond milk to the cooking liquid.

Serve in a bowl and add some warm milk or use almond milk for a dairy-free alternative.

Savory Quinoa

Ingredients:
1 cup quinoa
2 cups water
2 tsp ghee
¾ tsp sea salt
1 small cucumber peeled, seeded and cut into 1inch cubes
1 large heirloom tomato cut into 1 inch cubes
2 tbsp finely chopped cilantro
2 tsp finely chopped mint (leaves only)
1 tbsp finely chopped fresh dill
The juice of one lime
¼ tsp black pepper
½ cup (packed) baby spinach leaves

Preparation:
Soak the quinoa in three cups of water for thirty minutes. Rinse and wash again and drain completely in a fine mesh strainer. In a medium-sized pot, heat the ghee on medium heat and add the washed and drained quinoa. Sauté for about thirty seconds. Add the water and bring to a boil. Add the salt and bring to a boil. Place a tight-fitting lid on the pot and cook on low heat for 18-20 minutes.

Open the lid and fluff with a fork. Let it cool completely. Now add the rest of the ingredients and mix well. Serve at room temperature.

Lime Rice

Ingredients:
1 white Basmati rice
2 cups water
1½ tsp salt
3 tbsp oil
1 tsp mustard seeds
¼ tsp turmeric
½ tsp black pepper
10 cashews coarsely chopped
¼ cup fresh or dry unsweetened shredded coconut
Juice of 1 lime
3 tbsp chopped cilantro

Preparation:
Wash the rice in three changes of water and drain completely. Place the rice, water and salt in a medium sized pot and bring to a boil. Turn the heat down to low and place a tight-fitting lid and cook for 15 minutes. Keep aside. Heat oil and add the mustard seeds. Cover with a lid as they pop. After they pop, add the cashews, turmeric and black pepper. Sauté for about 30 seconds. Then add the coconut, lime juice and cilantro to the cooked rice. Mix well and serve warm.

Flatbread Crackers

Ingredients:
1¾ cups spelt flour
1 tbsp chopped rosemary plus 2 (6-inch) sprigs or 2 tbsp seeds such as poppy and sesame and caraway seeds
1 tsp baking powder
¾ tsp salt
½ cup water
1/3 cup olive oil plus more for brushing
Flaky sea salt (optional)

Preparation:
Preheat oven to 450°F with a baking sheet on the middle rack. Stir together flour, chopped rosemary, baking powder, and salt in a medium bowl. Make a well in center, then add water and oil and gradually stir into flour with a wooden spoon until a dough forms. Knead dough gently on a work surface 4 or 5 times. Divide dough into 3 pieces and roll out 1 piece (keep remaining pieces covered with plastic wrap) on a sheet of parchment paper into a 10-inch round (making sure the dough is rolled thin).

Lightly brush top with additional oil and scatter small clusters of rosemary leaves or seeds on top, pressing in slightly. Sprinkle with sea salt. Slide rolled dough (still on parchment) onto preheated baking sheet and bake until pale golden and browned in spots, 8 to 10 minutes.

Transfer flatbread to a rack to cool, then make 2 more rounds (1 at a time) on fresh parchment (do not oil or salt until just before baking). Gently break the flatbread into pieces. Flatbread can be made 2 days ahead and cooled completely, and stored in an airtight container at room temperature.

Corn and Bell Pepper With Rice

Ingredients:
1 ear of corn de-husked
3 tbsp oil
½ tsp turmeric
2 cloves of garlic finely chopped
1 red pepper deseeded and cut into 1 inch pieces
1 cup of brown rice
2 cups of water
1 tsp salt
¼ tsp salt
1 tsp black pepper

Preparation:
Roast the corn on the stove top on all sides till golden brown. Let it cool and then remove the corn with a sharp knife. Wash the rice in three changes of water and drain completely. Place the rice, 1 tsp of salt and water in a medium sized pot and bring to a rapid boil. Place a tight-fitting lid and cook on low heat for 35 minutes. In the meanwhile, heat the oil and add the garlic and turmeric. Saute for 1 minute. Now add the red pepper, salt and pepper and sauté on high heat for 3 minutes. Now add the corn and the rice and sauté or 4-5 minutes. Serve warm.

Quinoa with Coconut and Lime

Ingredients:
1 cup quinoa washed and soaked in 3 cups of water for 30 minutes
3 tbsp oil
1 tsp mustard seeds
A pinch of hing (asafetida)
2 dried red chilies broken in half and seeds discarded
1 tsp grated ginger
½ tsp turmeric
10 cashews
2 cups of water
1 ¼ tsp salt
3 tbsp chopped cilantro
5 tbsp freshly grated or unsweetened dry shredded coconut
The juice of 1 lime

Preparation;
Drain the soaked quinoa and wash and drain completely. Heat the oil and add the mustard seeds and cover with a lid. When they stop popping, add the hing, red chilies, ginger, turmeric and cashews and cook for about 1 minute. Now add the drained quinoa, salt and water. Bring to a boil, cover with a tight-fitting lid and cook on low heat for 18-20 minutes. Now add the cilantro, coconut and lime juice and serve warm.

Grains

Moong (Mung) Dal Pancakes

Ingredients:
1 cup moong dal soaked in 4 cups
  of water for 4 hours
½ cup of water
½ jalapeno chopped finely
¼ inch tsp grated ginger
½ tsp cumin seeds
½ tsp salt
6 tbsp of oil

Preparation:
Drain the soaked dal and wash in three
changes of water. Drain completely.
Blend the dal, jalapeno, and ginger
together with ⅛ cup of water. As you
grind the dal, it should have the consistency of pancake batter. Mix the salt and
cumin seeds in the batter. Add the rest
of the water and mix well.

Heat a cast iron skillet on medium heat.
Check the readiness of the skillet by
adding a few drops of water. If it sizzles
and evaporates, it is ready. Next pour
about 1/4 cup of batter in the center of
the skillet and spread evenly with the
back of a spoon. Starting from the center, using gentle pressure, spiral outwards
until the dough is spread evenly. Drizzle
1 tsp of oil on the dosa andcook for 3-4
minutes. Flip the dosa and cook for 1
minute. Stack them on a plate. You will
make 6 dosas. The original side should
have a golden brown color and have
a crisp texture. Serve with any of the
chutneys featured in this book.

Dosa

Ingredients:
1½ cups brown basmati rice
¾ cup urad dal (black lentils
  without the skin)
1 tsp salt
3 tsp methi seeds (fenugreek)
1¼ cups of water
10 tsp oil

Preparation:
Soak rice, urad dal in 4 cups of water.
Soak the methi seeds in ½ cup of water
overnight. Wash and drain the rice and
dal in three changes of water. Drain
completely. Grind rice, dal and methi
seeds together with water in two batches
if necessary. Pour the batter into a large
bowl and add 1 tsp salt and mix well.
Keep the batter in a warm place so it can
ferment overnight. Before making dosas,
mix the batter again. You will know the
dough has fermented when you see tiny
bubbles in the batter as well as a slightly
sour smell.

Heat a cast iron skillet on medium heat.
Check the readiness of the skillet by
adding a few drops of water. If it sizzles
and evaporates, it is ready. Next pour
about ¼ cup of batter in the center of
the skillet and spread evenly with the
back of a spoon. Starting from the center, using gentle pressure, spiral outwards
until the dough is spread evenly. Drizzle
1 tsp of oil on the dosa and flip it about
3-4 minutes later. After you flip it, cook
for 1 minute. Stack them on a plate.

You will make about 10 dosas. The
original side should have a golden
brown color and have a crisp texture.
Serve with any of the chutneys featured
in this book.

Spelt Flatbread with Fresh Fenugreek

Ingredients:
1 cup organic spelt flour
¼ cup water
1 bunch fresh fenugreek, leaves
  only (or spinach)
½ tsp cumin powder
½ tsp turmeric
½ tsp salt
1 tbsp oil
Ghee for smearing

Preparation:
Wash and drain the fenugreek leaves
thoroughly. Finely chop the leaves and
add it to the flour and salt in a mixing
bowl. Also add the cumin powder and
turmeric and slowly add the water.
Mix with your hands till dough is
formed. Once the dough ball comes
together, add the oil and knead it for
about 4 minutes.

Cover the bowl and let it rest for 20
minutes. If at this point the dough
seems too sticky, add 2 tbsp of flour and
knead gently. Heat a cast iron skillet.
In the meanwhile, make a 2 inch ball
of the dough and roll it out into a thin
and even disk about 4-5 inches in
diameter. Cook on the griddle till it
begins to puff up gently. Turn it over
and cook on the other side.

Place the bread in a container with a lid and drizzle about one tsp of ghee on the flatbread. Keep it covered so they remain soft. Continue with the dough till all breads are cooked. Yield: 6

Savory Semolina

Ingredients:
1 cup semolina
4 tbsp oil
1 tsp mustard seeds
A pinch of hing (asafetida)
½ tsp turmeric
2 dry red chilies broken in half and seeds discarded
10 whole cashews chopped coarsely
1 tsp grated ginger
¼ cup thinly sliced green beans
¼ cup finely diced carrots
¼ cup finely shredded cabbage
1¾ tsp salt
3½ cups of water
½ cup freshly grated coconut or ¼ cup dry unsweetened shredded coconut
4 tbsp chopped cilantro
The juice of 1 lime

Preparation:
Roast the semolina in a skillet without any oil for about 12-14 minutes on medium low heat. Stir constantly to avoid burning. When the semolina is fragrant, turn off the heat and keep aside. In a large pot, heat the oil and add the mustard seeds. Cover it partially with a lid and once the seeds stop popping, add the red chilies, asafetida, ginger and the cashews. Cook for 1 minute. Now add the vegetables and cook on high heat for 3-4 minutes. Now add the salt and water

and bring to a boil. When the water starts boiling, slowly add the semolina and whisk constantly to avoid lumps. Be careful of being splattered by the very hot semolina. Once everything is mixed well, cover with a lid and steam for 2-3 minutes. Mix well and garnish with the coconut, cilantro and lime. Drizzle a tsp of ghee in each bowl before serving

Rice with Raw Mango

Ingredients:
1 cup white basmati rice
2 cups of water
1 tsp salt
¼ cup of grated raw mango (do not grate the skin)
¾ cup of freshly grated or dry unsweetened shredded coconut
2 red chilies broken in half and seeds discarded
½ tsp mustard seeds
½ tsp turmeric
¼ cup of water or a bit more as needed
2 tbsp ghee
10 cashews
15 curry leaves

Preparation:
Wash the rice in three changes of water and drain completely. Place the washed rice, the measured water and salt in a medium-sized pot and bring to a rapid boil. Cover with a tight-fitting lid and turn the heat down to low. Cook for 15 minutes and let it rest for 5 minutes. Now spread the rice on a cookie sheet to cool. In the meanwhile, grind the raw mango, coconut, chilies, mustard seeds and turmeric to a fine paste with very

little water. The paste needs to be thick, so add very little water. Heat the ghee and add the cashews and curry leaves and fry for 1 minute. Add this to the rice, along with the mango paste and mix well. Serve warm or at room temperature.

Sarah's Greek Couscous

Ingredients:
1 cup couscous
1¼cups water
1 small cucumber peeled, seeded and diced
10 cherry or grape tomatoes halved
½ cup feta cheese crumbled
1 tbsp chopped fresh oregano
4 tbsp extra virgin olive oil
The juice of 2 lemons
8 kalamata olives
¾ tsp salt
½ tsp pepper

Preparation:
Boil the water and add the couscous and salt and cover with a tight-fitting lid and turn off the heat. Let it sit for 10 minutes. Open and fluff with a fork and let it cool completely. In another bowl, add the cucumbers, tomatoes, olives, feta cheese, olive oil, lemon juice, oregano and pepper. When the couscous has completely cooled down, add it to the bowl with the vegetables. Serve at room temperature.

Couscous with Green Vegetables

Ingredients:
1 tbsp ghee
1 cup couscous
1¼ cups of water
1 tsp salt
1 tbsp ghee
2 cloves of garlic finely chopped
10 green beans stringed and cut into 2 inch pieces
15-20 snow peas stringed and cut into 1 inch pieces
1 small zucchini cut into 1 inch cubes
¾ tsp salt
1 tsp pepper
The juice of 1 lemon
A few leaves of mint

Preparation:
Boil the water and pour the couscous, salt and ghee in the pot. Turn off the heat and mix well and cover with a lid and let it sit for 10 minutes. In the meanwhile, heat the ghee, and add the garlic and cook for about 1 minute. Now add the vegetables, salt and pepper and sauté on high heat for about 5 minutes. Cover with a tight-fitting lid and steam for about 3 minutes. Add the cooked vegetables with the couscous and fluff with a fork. Add the lemon juice and mint leaves and serve warm.

General Maurel's Asian Noodles

Ingredients:
6 tbsp sunflower oil
½ cup Braggs
¼ cup rice wine vinegar
2 tbsp cornstarch
1 clove garlic finely chopped
1 tsp grated ginger
1 small red onion thinly sliced
2 medium carrots thinly sliced
2 stalks celery, thinly sliced
1 lb extra firm tofu, cut into one inch cubes
4 baby bok choy cut into strips
14 oz rice noodles
3 tbsp toasted black sesame seeds

Preparation:
Heat a small skillet and dry toast the sesame seeds till fragrant on medium low heat. This should take 3-4 minutes. Keep aside. Heat the oil in a large pan and add the onions garlic, ginger, and tofu and cook for 4-5 minutes. Now add the carrots and celery and cook for 3-4 minutes.

Mix Braggs and rice wine vinegar in a small bowl and whisk in the corn starch. Add to sauteed vegetables. Heat and stir until liquid turns into a thick sauce. Add bok choy and cook for only 1 minute. Turn off the heat. In the meantime, boil 6 cups of water and add the rice noodles and cook according to directions on package. Drain the noodles and add to the vegetables and mix well. Serve immediately.

Coconut Rice

Ingredients:
1 cup white Basmati rice
2 cups of water
1½ tsp salt
¾ cup fresh or dry unsweetened shredded coconut
2 tbsp oil
1 tsp mustard seeds
A generous pinch of hing (asafetida)
3 red chilies broken in half and seed discarded
10 fresh curry leaves (optional)
8-10 cashews coarsely chopped

Preparation:
Wash the rice in three changes of water and drain completely. In a medium sized pot, add 2 cups of water and salt and bring to a boil. When it boils rapidly, place a tight-fitting lid and cook on low heat for 15 minutes. Allow the rice to cool for about 10 minutes and gently break apart the lumps and add the coconut to it. Keep aside.

Heat oil and add the mustard seeds. Place a lid and and after they pop, add the cashews, hing, curry leaves and red chilies. Stir fry till the cashews turn golden brown. Add the spice mix to the rice and mix well. Mix well and serve at room temperature.

Legumes and Beans

Legumes are classified as lentils, beans, or peas, are all seeds from specific plants. Legumes have been cultivated for thousands of years. In fact, moong or mung beans are mentioned in 5,000 year old Ayurvedic texts. The diet of many cultures around the world features legumes and beans for its dense nutrition — high in complex carbohydrates, protein and fiber. Legumes are a rich source of protein for vegetarians. According to Ayurveda, legumes are astringent in taste. They help build all the seven dhatus, especially muscle tissue, thus making is an important addition to a vegetarian diet.

Legumes are part of almost every meal in vedic cooking. The protein in legumes is easier to digest than meat products, cheese, eggs, and fish. Protein from legumes require some effort to digest and those new to vegetarianism will find it very helpful to use spices that help digestion such as asafetida, cumin, fresh ginger, fennel, and black pepper. It is vital to soak beans overnight and it is important to wash them thoroughly and add fresh water to begin cooking. Removing the foam and scum during cooking is another way to reduce gassiness. Lastly, using the appropriate spices and simmering them with lentils or beans is also important for optimal digestion.

Punjabi Dal

Ingredients:

1 cup red lentils
3 cups water
2 tbsp ghee or oil
1 tsp ginger grated
½ tsp turmeric
1 tsp cumin powder
1½ tbsp coriander powder
¼ tsp cayenne powder
1 medium tomato finely chopped
1 tsp salt

Preparation:

Wash the lentils in three changes of water. Then add the three cups of water and bring to a boil. Skim the foam off the top and cook for about 15 minutes or till the lentils are fully cooked. In the meanwhile, heat the ghee and sauté the ginger, turmeric, cumin powder and coriander powder for about 1 minute. Cook the tomato on medium heat for five minutes till it is completely soft. Then add to the cooked lentils and simmer for five minutes. Serve warm.

Coconut Flavored Dal

Ingredients:

1 cup moong dal
3 cups water
½ can coconut milk
1 tsp ghee
½ tsp cumin powder
½ tsp turmeric
¾ tsp salt
The juice of 1 lime

Preparation:

Wash the moong dal in three changes of water. Add the water and bring to a boil. Skim off any foam that rises to the surface. When the dal is almost cooked, add the salt and coconut milk. Let it simmer while you heat the ghee. Sauté the cumin and turmeric for about 45 seconds in the ghee and add it to the dal and simmer for about 5 minutes. Just before serving, add the lime juice.

Legumes and Beans

Sprouted Moong Beans

Ingredients:
1 cup dry moong beans
3-4 cups water
2 tbsp oil
1 tsp mustard seeds
A generous pinch of hing (asafetida)
3 dry red chilies
½ tsp turmeric
½ tsp grated ginger
1 tsp salt
The juice of 1 lime
4 tbsp shredded dry unsweetened coconut
4 tbsp chopped cilantro

Preparation:
Soak the beans overnight. The next morning, drain completely and wash the beans. Drain again and place in a colander with a towel on top. Let this sit in a warm spot for 24 hours or more (depending on how cool the weather is). You will begin to see little tails on the beans. This means the sprouting process has begun. The sprouts are ready to be used when they are about ½ inch to one inch long. Now the beans will have increased in volume. So add 5 -7 cups of water to the sprouts and bring to a boil. You will notice that the skins will begin to float on top. Carefully skim off as much of the skin as possible and discard.

The beans will require about 25-30 minutes of cooking on medium heat with the lid on. Continue to skim off the skins as much as possible. In the meanwhile, heat the oil in a small skillet. Break the chilies in half and shake well to discard the seeds. Add the mustard seeds and place lid on it. Once the mustard seeds finish popping, add the chilies, hing, turmeric and ginger and sauté for about 45 seconds. Add this spice mixture to the cooked beans along with the salt. Bring to a boil. By now most of the water from the beans will have evaporated. Simmer on medium for about six minutes. Add the coconut, cilantro and lime juice just before serving.

Blackeyed Peas

Ingredients:
1 cup blackeyed peas soaked in 4 cups of water overnight
2 tbsp oil
1 cinnamon stick
1 small onion finely chopped
½ tsp grated ginger
1 clove garlic finely chopped
1 tsp turmeric
1 tsp cumin powder
2 tbsp coriander powder
½ tsp cayenne powder
3 medium tomatoes finely chopped
2 tsp salt
2 tbsp finely chopped cilantro

Preparation:
Drain the soaked beans and wash thoroughly. Add 4-5 cups of water and bring to a boil. Skim off any foam and scum. Continue to cook on medium heat till the beans are tender. In the meanwhile, heat the oil and add the cinnamon stick and onion and sauté on medium heat till light brown. Then add the ginger and garlic and cook for about a minute.

Now add the spices and sauté for one minute. Add the chopped tomatoes and stir fry for about 10-13 minutes or till the tomatoes are completely soft. Add the cooked beans along with the salt and bring to a boil. Simmer for 10 minutes so the spices can infuse the beans. Add the cilantro just before serving.

Dal

Ingredients:

1 cup red lentils
3½ cups of water
2 tbsp extra virgin oil or ghee
1 tsp mustard seeds
A pinch of hing (asafetida)
1 tsp cumin seeds
1 tsp grated or finely chopped ginger
½ tsp turmeric
1 Roma tomato finely chopped
1 tsp salt
½ tsp black pepper
2 tbsp dry unsweetened
   shredded coconut
Juice of 1 lime
4 tbsp cilantro

Preparation:

Wash the lentils in three changes of water. Place the lentils and water in a medium sized pot and bring to a boil. Skim the froth as it rises to the surface and discard. Cook on medium heat till the lentils are soft and fully cooked about 15 minutes. In a small pan, heat the oil and add the mustard seeds and allow them to pop. Next add the cumin seeds and ginger and sauté for about 45 seconds. Add the hing and turmeric and sauté for 10 seconds. Add this to the cooked dal along with salt and pepper. Bring the dal to a boil and simmer for 5 minutes. Add cilantro, coconut and lime juice and serve hot.

White Bean Soup

Ingredients:

1 cup white beans soaked overnight in 4 cups water
3 tbsp oil
1 leek washed and thinly sliced (only the white part)
1 tsp dried rosemary
1 tsp grated ginger
2 medium carrots thinly sliced
4 sticks celery thinly sliced
1½ tsp cumin powder
2 tbsp coriander powder
2 tbsp fennel powder
½ tsp turmeric
2 tsp salt
½ tsp black pepper
1 bunch cilantro finely chopped
The juice of 2 limes (optional)

Preparation:

Wash the soaked beans and drain completely. Add 5 cups of water and the beans to a large pot and bring to a boil. Skim any foam off from the top and discard. After it begins boiling, reduce the heat to medium and cook for about 60-75 minutes. In the meanwhile, heat the oil and sauté the vegetables and spices together for about 5 minutes. When the beans are almost cooked, add the vegetables and salt and cook till they are tender. Add the cilantro and lime juice just before serving.

Hummus

Ingredients:

½ cup garbanzo beans
3 cups of water
1 large clove of garlic crushed
3 tbsp olive oil
2 tbsp tahini
¾ tsp salt
¼ tsp pepper
The juice of 2 lemons

Preparation:

Soak the garbanzo beans overnight in 3 cups of water. Wash and drain completely and cook with 3 cups of fresh water till soft and tender. Save ⅓ cup of the cooking water and drain the beans. Allow it to cool and then place all the ingredients in a blender or food processor and blend till smooth. Serve with fresh vegetables or pita bread.

Legumes and Beans

Dal Soup

Ingredients:
1 cup split chick peas (chana dal)
3 cups water
2 tbsp oil
1 tsp mustard seeds
A pinch of hing
1 tsp cumin powder
½ tsp turmeric
¼ tsp cayenne
½ tsp fennel seed powder
2 tsp coriander powder
1 tsp grated ginger
1 yellow squash chopped into
   one inch cubes
1½ tsp salt

Preparation:
Soak the dal overnight in 4 cups of water. Drain it and wash in three changes of water and drain completely. Add 3 cups of fresh water and bring to a boil. Skim the foam off the top and cook on medium heat for about 25-30minutes. To save time and energy, place a lid on it partially.

Meanwhile, heat the oil and add the mustard seeds. Cover it with a lid and after they pop, add hing, cumin, turmeric, fennel, coriander and ginger. Sauté for about 45 seconds. Then add the squash and cook for about 3 minutes. Add this spice-vegetable mix into the cooked dal along with the salt and simmer for about 5 minutes.

Spinach Dal

Ingredients:
1 cup red lentils
3 cups water
2 tbsp oil
A pinch of hing
1 tsp cumin powder
2 tbsp coriander powder
½ tsp turmeric
½ tsp cayenne or black pepper
2 bunches spinach washed
   and chopped coarsely
1½ tsp salt

Preparation:
Wash the dal in three changes of water and drain completely. Now add 3 cups of fresh water and bring to a boil. Skim the foam off the top and cook on medium heat till soft. This should take about 15 minutes. To save time and energy, place a lid on it partially.

Wash the spinach carefully and chop coarsely. Meanwhile, heat the oil and add the spice mix and sauté for about 30 seconds. Add the chopped spinach and sauté for 3 minutes. Add to the cooked dal along with the salt and simmer for 2 minutes.

Dal with Cardamom and Bay Leaves

Ingredients:
1 cup red lentils
3 cups of water
2 tbsp oil
2 bay leaves
3 cardamom pods
½ small onion finely chopped
1 clove of garlic finely chopped
1 tbsp Tridoshic spice blend
   (see spice chapter)
1 medium tomato finely chopped
1½ tsp salt
2 tbsp chopped cilantro

Preparation:
Wash and drain the lentils in three changes of water. Add the 3 cups of water and bring to a boil. Remove any foamy scum from the top and discard. Cook the lentils for 15 minutes. In the meanwhile, heat the oil in a small pan and add the bay leaves and cardamom pods. Saute for about 45 seconds.

Now add the onion and cook on medium heat till it is golden brown. Add the garlic and the spice blend. Saute for about 45 seconds. Next add the tomato cook the mixture for about 4-5 minutes. When the tomato is soft, add it to the cooked lentils along with the salt and bring to a boil. Simmer for 8-10 minutes. Add the chopped cilantro just before serving.

Kidney Beans

Ingredients:
1 cup kidney beans
4 cups water
2 tbsp oil
1 tsp grated ginger
1 tbsp fennel seeds
¾ tsp cayenne
2 tbsp coriander powder
1tsp cumin powder
3 medium tomatoes finely chopped
1¾ tsp salt

Preparation:
Soak the kidney beans in 5 cups of water overnight. The following day, wash and drain the beans completely. Now add 4 cups of fresh water and bring to a boil. As it cooks, skim off any foamy scum cook for about 45-55 minutes on medium heat. To save energy and time, cover partially with a lid.

In the meanwhile, heat the oil in a medium sized pan and add the ginger and fennel seeds. Cook for about 45 seconds. Now add the spice powders cook for another 45 seconds. Next add the tomatoes and cook on medium heat till they are soft. Now add the tomato mixture to the cooked beans along with the salt and simmer for 8-10 minutes.

Garbanzo Beans

Ingredients:
1 cup garbanzo beans
4 cups water
2 tbsp oil
1 small onion finely chopped
½ tsp grated ginger
1 clove garlic finely chopped
1 tsp turmeric
1 tsp cumin powder
2 tbsp coriander powder
¼ tsp cayenne powder
3 medium tomatoes finely chopped
1¾ tsp salt
2 tbsp finely chopped cilantro

Preparation:
Soak the garbanzo beans in 5 cups of water overnight. The following day, wash and drain the beans completely. Now add 4 cups of fresh water and bring to a boil. As it cooks, skim off any foamy scum cook for about 45-55 minutes on medium heat. To save energy and time, cover partially with a lid.

Heat the oil and add the onion and sauté on medium heat till light brown. Then add the ginger and garlic and cook for about a minute. Now add the spices and sauté for one minute. Add the chopped tomatoes and stir fry for about 10-13 minutes or till the tomatoes are completely soft. Add this mix to the beans along with the salt and bring to a boil. Simmer for 10 minutes so the spices can infuse the beans. Add the cilantro just before serving.

Desserts

Life is uncertain. Eat dessert first. ~ERNESTINE ULMER

Even if you disagree with this quote, you will be thrilled to know that Ayurveda does support eating dessert first. Why? Because our digestive "agni" is strongest at the beginning of the meal your chances of creating toxins or "ama" are reduced. So if you feel inclined to have dessert first, go ahead! Ayurveda approves! Sweet foods evoke joy, bliss and happiness in us. In fact, sweetness is our inherent nature. In India it is said that serving sweets during celebrations is a way to remind ourselves of our true nature. In this dessert section, the most saatvic and pure ingredients are used. Ojas producing foods such as pears, ghee, milk, raisins, saffron and coconut are featured in many recipes.

Warm Sautéed Pears

Ingredients:
4 ripe D' Anjou pears
2 tbsp ghee
3 tbsp turbinado sugar
½ tsp ground ginger
¾ tsp cinnamon
1/8 tsp salt

Optional:
Vanilla ice cream and 3 tbsp
slivered almonds

Preparation:
Peel the pears and cut them in half lengthwise and then cut into four pieces. Heat the ghee in a skillet and add the ginger, cinnamon, sugar, pears and salt. Saute the pears on medium high heat for about four minutes or till they are soft. Top with slivered almonds and vanilla ice cream and serve.

Cinnamon Sautéed Bananas

Ingredients
3 tbsp ghee
1 tsp cinnamon powder
5-6 strands of saffron
5 large bananas firm but ripe
3 tsp turbinado sugar
1 tbsp shredded dry
    unsweetened coconut

Preparation:
Peel the bananas, cut into crosswise slices ¼ inch thick, and keep aside. Heat the ghee in a skillet and add the cinnamon and saffron. Cook for about 30 seconds. Now add the bananas and sugar. Cook on medium heat for about 3 minutes or till the bananas are tender. Sprinkle the coconut and serve warm.

Tapioca Pudding

Ingredients:
½ cup tapioca pearls soaked for an hour
    in 2 cups of water
5-8 strands of saffron
2 cups of 2% or whole milk
½ cup turbinado cup sugar
2 tbsp slivered almonds
½ tsp cardamom powder

Preparation:
Cook tapioca in milk, saffron and the sugar on medium heat till soft, but not mushy. This will ensure that the starch is released from the tapioca to thicken the pudding. This will require frequent stirring. Then add almonds and cardamom powder and cook for another 4-5 minutes. Serve chilled with mango slices or fresh berries.

Carrot Halva

Ingredients:
1½ lb carrots grated
2 cups milk 2%
5 tbsp turbinado sugar
3 tbsp ghee
A small handful of raisins
6-8 almonds
1 tsp cardamom powder
1 tbsp rose water (optional)

Preparation:
Soak the almonds in one cup of water for 20 minutes. Peel the skin and chop coarsely. Keep aside. Place the grated carrots, raisins and milk in a large pot and bring to a boil. Add the sugar and stir often to make sure it does not stick. Once all the milk is absorbed into the carrots add the ghee, almonds and continue to cook for another 10 minutes. Finally add the cardamom powder and rose water if using and mix well. Serve warm or at room temperature.

Semolina Halva

Ingredients
½ cup semolina
4 tbsp ghee
1/3 cup turbinado sugar
2 cups water
5-8 strands of saffron
2 tbsp raisins
4 almonds blanched slivered and chopped coarsely
½ tsp cardamom powder
1 tbsp rose water (optional)

Preparation:
Boil the water with sugar and saffron in a pan over low medium heat and simmer. In the meanwhile, melt the ghee in a pot on medium heat. Add the semolina, raisins and almonds and roast to golden brown color; stirring constantly. This will take about 8-10 minutes. Add the sugar water slowly and carefully as it may splatter. Turn down the heat to medium low and let it cook for about 8 minutes stirring constantly till all the water is absorbed and the consistency is thick. Add the cardamom and rose water and serve warm.

Almond Halva

Ingredients:
1 cup almonds
1 cup 2% milk
2-3 tbsp ghee
½ cup turbinado sugar
5-8 strands of saffron

Preparation:
Soak and the almonds for about 2 hours and peel them. Place the almonds and the milk in a blender and grind to a fine paste. Cook this mixture in a heavy bottomed pan on medium low heat along with sugar and saffron till it becomes thick. Now stir in the ghee and cook for another 8-10 minutes. Serve warm.

Rice Pudding

Ingredients:
1 tbsp ghee
1 handful white Basmati rice
6-8 strands of saffron
A small handful of raisins
¼ cup slivered almonds
3 cups organic whole milk
¼ cup turbinado sugar or
    more if desired
½ tsp cardamom powder

Preparation:
Wash the rice in two changes of water and drain completely. Heat the ghee and add the rice and sauté on medium heat for 3-4 minutes. Then add the saffron and raisins and almonds and sauté for two minutes. Now add the sugar and milk and bring to a boil. Simmer for 45 minutes stirring often till it becomes creamy. Scrape the bottom of the pot often so it does not stick and burn. Stir in the cardamom powder and serve warm.

Desserts

Coconut milk Pudding with Fresh Berries

Ingredients:
2 cans of coconut milk
6 tbsp corn starch
¼ cup organic turbinado sugar
2 tsp vanilla
¼ tsp salt
10-12 strawberries, stems
    removed and cut in half

Preparation:
Place 1½ cans of the coconut milk in a medium pot on medium heat and bring to a gentle boil. Add the sugar, vanilla and salt. In the meanwhile, whisk the corn starch and the remaining ½ can of coconut milk together. Add it slowly to the hot coconut milk and whisk constantly till the coconut milk thickens. Constant stirring is necessary to avoid lumps. Pour the pudding into a glass dish and let it sit for 5 minutes. Then cover with plastic wrap and refrigerate for four hours to set. Top with berries and serve cold.

Alternatives:
Top with ripe mango or pineapple slices. Mandarin oranges also add a delightful dimension to this dessert.

Date Ladoos

Ingredients:
3 tbsp ghee
1 tsp cinnamon
15 medjool dates pitted and chopped coarsely
½ cup raisins
¼ cup coarsely chopped pistachios or cashews
¾ tsp cardamom powder
1 cup dry shredded unsweetened coconut

Preparation:
Heat the ghee in a large skillet. Add the cinnamon and cook for about 30 seconds. Now add the chopped dates, raisins and nuts and cook on medium low heat for about 8 minutes. As this mixture cooks, it is important that you use a potato masher to mash the dates and raisins together. Now add the cardamom and mix well. Allow the mixture to cool. Pour the coconut in a mixing bowl. Take about 2 tbsp of the date mix and roll into a ball. Then roll the ball in the shredded coconut. Do this with the rest of the mix and roll them in the coconut. You can store these in an air-tight container for a week or so.

Besan Ladoos

Ingredients:
1 ½ cups gram flour (besan)
2 tbsp fine semolina flour
¼ cup ghee
¾ cup sugar
4 tbsp sliced almonds
½ tsp cardamom powder

Preparation:
Place the besan, semolina and ghee in a medium pan and on medium heat. Begin roasting it till it turns golden brown. It is important to stir continuously to prevent burning. When the besan mix is roasted, you will also notice a sweet aroma. This should take about 7 to 10 minutes.

Allow the mix to cool down, but not cold. It must be lukewarm when you add the sugar, almonds and cardamom. To prepare the ladoos, take 2 tbsp of the warm mix in your palm and gently press to form a ball. Smooth it out as you go. Make all the ladoos in this way and allow it to cool completely. Store in an air-tight container for up to 2 weeks.

To Your Sweetness!

20310210R00024

Made in the USA
Charleston, SC
07 July 2013